Tasting
the Past

Tasting the Past

Recipes from
George III
to Victoria

JACQUI WOOD

Illustrations: Utro_na_more/iStockphoto

First published 2009, as part of *Tasting the Past: Recipes from the Stone Age to the Present*

This edition published 2019

The History Press
97 St George's Place, Cheltenham,
Gloucestershire, GL50 3QB
www.thehistorypress.co.uk

British Library Cataloguing in Publication Data.
A catalogue record for this book is available from the British Library.

ISBN 978 0 7509 9223 7

Typesetting and origination by The History Press
Printed and bound in Great Britain by TJ International Ltd.

Contents

Introduction

BRITISH FOOD has been hard to categorise in the past compared to the very distinctive cuisines of countries such as Italy, France and Germany. This is because it is an amalgamation of all of them, in the same way that the English language is a combination of five European languages: Celtic, Latin, Saxon, Viking and Norman. Our cuisine, too, is a combination of the typical foods of those that once conquered Britain over a thousand years ago.

But Britain's assimilation of the foods of other cultures did not stop after the Norman Conquest. During the medieval period, the spices brought from the Crusades by the Normans were used in almost every dish by those who could afford them. When Britain itself began to have colonies, the culinary embellishments to our diet began again. During the Elizabethan period, strange produce coming from the New World was also adopted with relish by our forbears.

The Civil War period introduced Puritan restrictions to our daily fare, making it against the law to eat a mince pie on Christmas Day because it was thought a decadent Papist tradition. The Georgians took on chocolate and coffee with gusto and even moulded their business transactions around the partaking of such beverages. But it was really not until the Victorian period – when it was said that the sun never set on the British Empire – that our diet became truly global in nature.

This book will hopefully become a manual for those readers who want to put on a themed dinner party, providing a wide selection of recipes from each period in history. I have not included those recipes that I feel you would never want to make, but instead have focused on dishes that will allow you to experience what it was really like to eat during those particular periods. No one, apart from the truly adventurous among you, is going to acquire a cow's udder from the butcher and stuff it as they did in the medieval period, or stuff a fish's stomach with chopped cod's liver!

Each chapter will begin with a brief introduction to the foods of the period that I found particularly fascinating during my research, and will end with the traditional festive food of the period. If you want to celebrate your Christmas in a completely different way, why not try a sumptuous Georgian banquet?

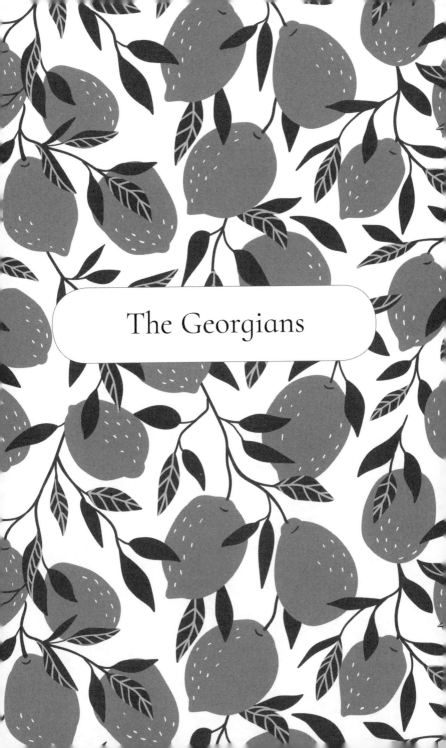

The Georgians

THINK OF THE ROYAL CRESCENT and Jane Austen centre in Bath and we have arrived at the Georgian period, characterised by genteel dances at assembly rooms, where mothers sought good suitors for their daughters. But outside that cosseted genteel world were the stirrings of the Industrial Revolution, and new towns were being built to house vast work forces that left their rural idyll for the riches of the towns. While there was always a large gap between the nobility and the peasantry, it was somehow becoming more palpable as they were both living in the same towns. Beggars would sit on frosty street corners and watch gilt carriages sweep past carrying ladies wrapped in furs. This movement to the towns also had a much greater effect on the food of the poor than had been seen in any other period. In the country, the farm worker at least had access to wild berries and nuts and an endless supply of root vegetables. In the towns, however, the factory workers crammed into their tiny terraced houses had no room to grow anything with which to supplement their basic diet.

There were also serious transport problems during this time, as the raw materials needed to manufacture their goods were brought to the new towns via muddy and badly maintained roads. More importantly, though, the labour force for the new factories also needed their food brought to them, and so the first canals were built in the to solve this problem. They also made it possible to transport delicate goods from the factories to the coastal ports. Josiah Wedgwood built his pottery works alongside these canals in order to transport his china without breakages throughout the country and onto ships at various ports.

At the other end of the scale, chocolate and coffee houses became the centres of fashionable social life. There were at one time over 500 in London alone. There were also chocolate and coffee houses for the supporters of various political parties: The Coco Tree Chocolate House for the Tories, for instance, and St James Coffee House for the Whigs. Alcoholic drinks were not served in these houses, but pipe smoking was very common. Coffee houses, however, went into decline in the mid-eighteenth century, as tea drinking became the universal British pastime. It was drunk in even the poorest homes throughout the land by the reign of George III. Tea was always drunk black at first, as it was in the countries it came from, until someone suggested that it could damage the stomach if drunk too frequently. And so it was suggested by medical men at the time that if a little milk was added to the tea, it would line the stomach and the drink could be enjoyed as frequently as desired.

This was also a time of great innovations in the kitchens of the stately homes, with the invention of a newly devised clockwork mechanism for turning the spit on which whole pigs or sheep were roasted. This device subsequently took the place of a poor kitchen worker, who would previously have spent all day manually turning those great spits whenever there was a great banquet planned. This period also saw the beginnings of the mass-produced oven. Until then, most people sent their pies to the local baker to have them cooked, as they had always done. But with the improved ironworks of the blossoming Industrial Revolution, ovens became more widely available.

The development of printing presses, too, introduced the middle classes to all manner of educational pursuits, of which cookbooks were one of the most popular. At first, the books were primarily the recipes of the famous French chefs of the time, who created gastronomic wonders for the aristocracy – dishes that the newly rich wanted to taste for themselves. But the war with France during the eighteenth century encouraged a new wave of patriotic cooking. Some of the well-known cookery writers of the day, such as Hanna Glasse, promoted good English cooking in her books. Her book, *The Art of Cookery Made Plain and Easy*, was said to have gone into at least 16 editions between 1747 and 1803.

Another fascinating development was the icehouse, many of which were being made in the country estates. I have been fascinated by these ever since I first heard about them, and have seen one or two in stately homes in Scotland. The idea was that great, underground, dome-roofed rooms were constructed and, when the lakes on the estate froze solid in the winter, the groundsmen would cut great chunks of ice from the lakes and stack it between layers of straw in the icehouses. Then, in the heat of the summer months, when the lady of the manor required delicate ices, she would order that ice was brought up to the kitchens. The ice was then crushed and mixed with salt to form a slush that was packed into double-skinned bowls, into which cream and custards were poured. With a little hard whipping by the cook, the icy walls of the bowl would turn it into ice cream for the guests at the dinner table. The ice never came into direct contact with the food, so it was actually very hygienic. These ice creams were very often married with the exotic fruits grown in the hot houses of the estate – a delight for all those privileged enough to eat it.

One of the most enduring culinary inventions in the world was said to have been invented during this period also, and that is the humble sandwich. Legend has it that John Montagu, 4th Earl of Sandwich, instructed his chef to devise such a snack. He was a keen gambler and, during a 24-hour card game marathon, he asked his chef to devise something for him to eat that required no fork or knife and that he could eat with one hand, while holding his cards with the other. The chef gave him a slice of meat between two pieces of toast, which fulfilled all the earl's requirements. This then became a popular snack in gambling circles and is now the world's most popular snack, eaten most frequently by people on the move.

Asparagus Omelette

1 bundle of fresh asparagus

6 eggs

50 g butter

Salt and pepper to taste

Parsley to garnish

Method

1. Boil the asparagus in water until it is tender.
2. Beat the eggs.
3. Melt the butter in the pan and add the eggs and the chopped, cooked asparagus.
4. Sprinkle the salt and pepper over it and cook until set.
5. Put on a plate and garnish with parsley before serving.

Potted Beef

All types of meat were potted at this time, not only to preserve them, but also so that dainty sandwiches could be made ready for teatime in wealthy ladies' parlours.

1 kg beef

100 g butter

4 tbsp flour

½ tsp salt

1 tsp ground cloves

2 tsp nutmeg

1 tin anchovy fillets

¼ tsp pepper

Method

1. Put the beef in a tight fitting dish with a lid.
2. Slice half the butter and put it on top of the meat.
3. Seal the dish with flour and water paste.
4. Bake in a slow oven for 3 hours or in a slow cooker for 4 hours.
5. Take the meat out and mince it in a food processor or hand mincer.
6. Add all the other ingredients, plus the fat from the stock in the pot, and mix well.
7. Press the mixture into small pots and cover with the rest of the butter, melted to seal the meat.

Oysters in Bread Rolls

4 dinner rolls
75 g butter
30 ml white wine
12 fresh oysters
2 tbsp finely chopped parsley

Method

1. Cut the tops off the rolls and scoop out the contents.
2. Brush the insides with melted butter.
3. Put the rolls in the oven until crisp.
4. Fry the oysters in the rest of the butter until cooked.
5. Add the wine and parsley to the pan and divide into the hot rolls, replacing the lid.

Battered Celery Hearts

5 or 6 small celery hearts

200 g flour

¼ tsp nutmeg

A small glass of wine

2 egg yolks

1 tsp salt

50 g butter

Method

1. Make the batter with the egg yolks, flour, nutmeg and wine.
2. Cut the celery hearts in half and boil in water until they are almost cooked.
3. Drain well and pat dry.
4. Dip each piece in the batter and shallow fry on all sides in butter.
5. When cooked, pour melted butter over the battered hearts and serve.

Beetroot Pancakes

200 g peeled, cooked
beetroot (if buying
pre-packaged, make sure
there is no vinegar on it)

40 ml brandy

4 tbsp double cream

4 egg yolks

150 g flour

2 tbsp sugar

Butter

½ tsp nutmeg

Method

1. Mash the beetroot well (if you have a ricer, all the better).
2. Mix with all the other ingredients, apart from the butter.
3. Melt the butter in a shallow pan, and when it is hot, drop spoonfuls of the mixture into it (about the size of a small, round cracker).
4. Turn when they start to bubble. These are equally good hot or cold, and very good with horseradish sauce.

English Rarebit

2 thick slices of brown bread
Small glass of red wine
225 g cheddar cheese

Method

1. Toast the bread.
2. Put it in a shallow dish and pour over the red wine.
3. Slice the cheese and place it in a thick layer over the bread.
4. Put it in the oven until the cheese has melted and gone golden brown.

Ragoo of Pigs' Ears

4 pig ears

2 glasses of wine

2 glasses of water

1 tbsp flour

50 g butter

1 anchovy, finely chopped

4 shallots, finely chopped

1 tsp English mustard

Salt to taste

Juice of 1 lemon

Method

1. Boil the ears in the water and wine until tender.
2. Drain, saving the stock, and cut the ears into slices.
3. Sprinkle the flour in the stock and bring to the boil to thicken.
4. Fry the pork slices in the butter until brown.
5. Add the stock and the rest of the ingredients to the pan and simmer.
6. Serve at once with fresh bread.

Beef Stew

2 rump steaks

Salt and pepper to taste

300 ml water

1 blade of mace

3 cloves

A bundle of sweet herbs
(parsley, thyme, savoury,
marjoram)

1 anchovy fillet

50 g butter

50 g flour

150 ml white wine

1 onion, quartered

10 oysters

Flour for dusting

50 g butter for frying

Method

1. In a pan, lay the steaks and cover with the rest of the ingredients (apart from the oysters, flour for dusting and the butter for frying).
2. Cover and stew until the steaks are tender.
3. Take the steaks out of the pan, dust them with flour, and fry them in the butter until brown.
4. Strain the gravy and pour it into the pan. Toss the steaks in it until hot and thickened.
5. Add the oysters and cook for 5 minutes in gravy.
6. Pour into a dish and garnish with pickle.

Three Ways to Serve Fried Sausages: Dish 1

225 g sausages

6 apples

Method

1. Peel and core the apples. Slice four thickly and quarter the other two.
2. Fry the sausages in a pan with the sliced and quartered apples.
3. Serve the sausages in a dish with the apples all around them. Garnish with the apple quarters.

Three Ways to Serve Fried Sausages: Dish 2

225 g sausages
225 g cabbage, sliced and boiled

Method

1. Fry the sausages in a pan and put to one side, keeping them warm.
2. Fry the cabbage in the sausage fat until it is browning on the bottom. Stir well and put into a dish topped with the sausages.

Three Ways to Serve Fried Sausages: Dish 3

225 g sausages
400 g cold Pease pudding
(made with dried peas, stock
and onions)

Method

1. Fry the sausages and keep warm.
2. Fry the Pease pudding in the sausage fat until it browns. Stir well and put into a dish.
3. Stick the sausages into the Pease pudding and serve.

Breaded Ham

It is interesting to note that breaded ham recipes have not changed much since the Georgian period.

1 large ham

2 beaten eggs

150 g breadcrumbs

75 g melted butter

Method

1. Soak the ham overnight in water if it is smoked and then change the water.
2. Boil the ham for the time required on the label.
3. Take the ham out and pull off the skin. Coat it with the egg and then the breadcrumbs, and pour the melted butter evenly over it.
4. Bake for a further 30 minutes in the oven.

Salmagundi

This dish would be a main meal salad today, but in the Georgian period it was a side dish or middle dish for supper.

The meat from 2 roast chickens, minced well

6 hard-boiled eggs (yolks and whites minced separately)

3 lemons, peeled and sliced finely

1 tin of anchovies

A bunch sorrel leaves

300 g spinach

4 sliced shallots

2 oranges, sliced thinly

1 tbsp horseradish, grated (you can use the horseradish in a jar, but not the creamed variety)

3 tbsp oil

Juice of 1 lemon

1 tsp mustard

Salt to taste

Method

1. On a large platter, spread a layer of the minced chicken.
2. Then place over the chicken a layer of minced egg yolks, a layer of anchovies, and a layer of minced egg whites.
3. Put the slices of lemon on top, and then a layer of sorrel and spinach (uncooked).
4. Top the spinach with the sliced shallots and finally with the sliced oranges.
5. Make the dressing by mixing the oil and lemon juice with the mustard and salt.
6. Pour this over the oranges and garnish with the horseradish.
7. The salmagundi can then be sliced from the top in wedges and served on small plates.

Cheshire Pork Pie

450 g loin of pork
½ tsp salt
¼ tsp nutmeg
¼ tsp pepper
4 eating apples, peeled, cored and sliced
1 tsp sugar
300 ml white wine
75 g butter
2 pig trotters for jelly
Hot water pastry

Method

1. With the pastry, mould the base and sides of your pie using your hands.
2. Cut the pork into steaks and rub with the spice and seasoning.
3. Lay half the pork loin on the bottom of the pie dish.
4. Put in a layer of sliced apples and sprinkle with sugar.
5. Put the remaining pork on top of the apples.
6. Pour the wine on top and dot with the butter. Put on the pie lid, sealing it well with water.
7. Bake in a moderate oven for 1 hour on a baking tray.
8. Put the trotters in a pan of water with some salt and boil well for 1 hour. Strain the stock and keep to one side.
9. When the pie is taken out of the oven, carefully make a hole in the lid and fill it with as much of the trotter stock as you can. Leave to cool (this stock will form the jelly traditionally seen in any pork pie). Serve cold.

Hot Water Crust Pastry

450 g plain flour

1 tsp salt

200 g lard

225 ml water and milk mixed
in equal quantities

Method

1. Mix the flour and salt together in a bowl.
2. Heat the milk and water in a pan with the lard until it boils.
3. Pour into the flour and beat well until smooth.
4. Let it go cold and then shape into the base and sides of your pie with your hands. Once filled, top with a lid and seal it.

A Fancy Dish of Herrings

12 small herrings

A large bunch of parsley

300 ml parsley sauce (made
with whole milk, parsley,
flour and butter)

100 g butter

50 g seasoned flour (just add
salt and pepper to it)

Method

1. In a large pan, melt the butter and dust the herring
   with flour. Fry until crisp on both sides. Set to one
   side and keep warm until they are all cooked.
2. Make the parsley sauce.
3. Fry the parsley in the same pan as the fish until it
   is crisp, but has not lost its colour.
4. Place a small, upturned cup in the middle of a large
   platter and surround it with the fried parsley.

5. Place the fish around the platter with their heads on the rim and their tails sticking up over the cup. The cup should be quite small, so that it does not stop the tails meeting each other. It should lift them slightly to bend them up.
6. Serve with parsley sauce.

Salmon Pie

1 whole salmon	
250 g gooseberries (frozen will do)	
1 tsp allspice	
¼ tsp black pepper	
½ tsp nutmeg	
1 tsp salt	
500 g puff pastry	
225 g butter	
25 g flour	

Method

1. Fillet the salmon and cut the fish into nice thick slices.
2. Boil half the gooseberries in enough water to cover until soft and strain, retaining the liquor.
3. When the gooseberry liquor is cold, brush each piece of salmon with it and rub in the spices and salt.

4. Put the fish (apart from 4 slices) into the bottom of a pastry-lined dish and cover with a pastry lid. Bake in a moderate oven for 1 hour.
5. While the salmon pie is cooking, boil the fish bones in water for 1 hour until reduced by half.
6. Melt half the butter in the pan and fry the rest of the salmon until the pieces are golden brown.
7. Add the strained fish stock to the fish and bring it to the boil. Simmer until thick.
8. Take the pie out of the oven and cut off the pastry lid.
9. Strain the gravy and add to it the other half of the gooseberries and butter.
10. Bring back to the boil and simmer for 10 minutes until the gooseberries are soft.
11. Pour this gravy and the fried salmon over the salmon in the pie and replace the lid. Set it aside to go cold.

Apple Fritters

4 large Cox's orange pippin
apples

1 glass of brandy

75 g sugar

1 tsp cinnamon

Peel of 1 lemon

50 g lard

3 tbsp flour

Method

1. Peel, pare and quarter the apples.
2. Put them in a dish with the brandy, sugar, lemon peel and the cinnamon.
3. Leave them overnight.
4. Take them out and dry them. Then dust them in flour and fry until golden in the lard.
5. Lay them in a dish covered with more sugar and serve with the brandy marinade in a jug.

Apple and Custard Pie

500 g puff pastry

4 large cooking apples

225 g sugar (this depends on
how sharp the apples are)

Lemon peel and juice

2 egg yolks

300 ml double cream

½ tsp nutmeg

1 blade of mace

Method

1. Line the sides of a dish with two thirds of the puff pastry.
2. Roll out the other third for the lid and put to one side.
3. Pare and quarter the apples and take out the cores.
4. Slice the apples and lay them in a thick row on the pastry.
5. Sprinkle over half the sugar.
6. Sprinkle with lemon peel and lemon juice.
7. Boil the peelings and core with the mace in a little water until they are soft and strain.
8. Pour this onto the apples and put on the pastry lid. Bake for 35 minutes in a hot oven.
9. Take the lid off the pie and put it carefully to one side, leaving the pie to cool.
10. Beat the egg yolks in the cream with the rest of the sugar.
11. Pour this custard on top of the apples in the pie and sprinkle with nutmeg.
12. Put the lid back on the pie and bake in a cool oven for 40 minutes until the custard is set.
13. Let the pie go cold before serving.

Fairy Butter

These were kept chilled until ready for use and eaten with wafers or plain cakes like a rich butter cream.

4 hard-boiled egg yolks

2 tbsp rosewater

50 g sugar

150 g unsalted butter

Method

1. Mash the egg yolks and mix with the other ingredients.
2. Press through a fine metal sieve until you have little ringlets of the butter.

Seedy Shortcake

These were very popular in Georgian times. Caraway seeds were used to help digestion, and this is still a proven remedy today.

225 g butter

225 g flour

1 egg

150 g sugar

1 tbsp caraway seeds

50 g raspberry jam

Method

1. Beat the butter until it is pale and soft. Add the sugar and then the egg.
2. Beat in the flour and caraway seeds.
3. Roll onto a floured board and use a wineglass as a cutter.
4. Place on a baking tray and prick them all over. Bake in a hot oven for 10 minutes until they turn a pale golden colour.
5. Serve hot, spread with raspberry jam.

Pistachio Cream

225 g pistachio nuts

300 ml cream

2 egg yolks

50 g sugar

50 g pistachio nuts, sliced
lengthways for decoration

Method

1. Shell the nuts and chop them. Put them, along with the cream, into a pan with the egg yolks and sugar mixed well together.
2. Stir over a gentle heat until thick, but do not let it boil.
3. Put it into a soup plate and let it go cold.
4. Decorate with the sliced nuts or surround it with red jelly. Serve immediately.

Sherry Trifle

This is close to our present-day version of the sherry trifle, in that there are three separate layers. It is definitely an adult dish, though, as there is a lot of wine and sherry in it!

225 g ratafia biscuits

1 glass sherry

300 ml cold custard

300 ml syllabub (made by beating double cream, sugar and wine together with lemon zest)

To garnish: flowers, crystallised fruits such as angelica and cherries

Method

1. Put the biscuits in a glass bowl and pour the sherry over them. Leave it to soak in.
2. Spread the cold custard on top and then put the syllabub on top of that.
3. Decorate with a selection of brightly coloured flowers and crystallised fruits.

Almond Hedgehog

This is good, but rather expensive to make, so halve the quantities if you have only a small party.

1 kg ground almonds

2 tbsp sherry

12 egg yolks

7 egg whites

600 ml cream

50 g sugar

225 g butter melted

150 g flaked almonds

1 packet of green jelly

Method

1. Mix the almonds with the sherry until it becomes a stiff paste. Beat in the egg yolks and whites.
2. Add the cream, sugar and melted butter.
3. Put in a pan and heat on a very gentle heat, stirring all the time until it is thick enough to form the shape of the hedgehog.
4. On a dish, shape the mixture into a hedgehog and stick it full of flaked almonds to resemble prickles.
5. Make the green jelly and, when cool, pour around the hedgehog.
6. When it is set, stick a few tops of rosemary stems into the jelly to make it look like grass.

Apricot Ice Cream

12 ripe, fresh apricots

175 g icing sugar

600 ml cream

A bowl full of ice and salt

A bowl with a lid on it

A jelly mould with lid

Method

1. Scald the apricots with boiling water and peel and chop them very finely.
2. Mix the sugar, cream and apricots together and put in the bowl with the lid on. Place this into a larger bowl filled with crushed ice and a handful of salt (this makes it slushy).
3. Check it every so often and stir well when the cream gets thick around the edges of your bowl.

4. When the cream is completely frozen, take it out of the bowl and press into a wet mould, putting the lid on when this is done.
5. Put the mould in the bowl of ice, covering it completely, and leave for 4 hours.
6. Serve immediately.

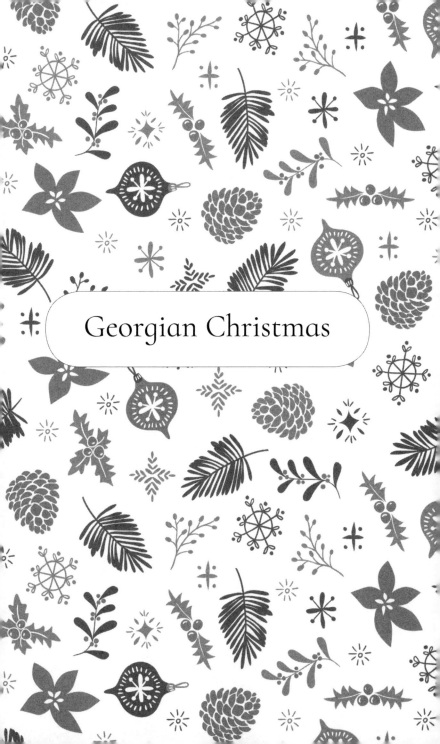

Georgian Christmas

Roast Turkey

7 kg turkey

Greaseproof paper

225 g butter

Chestnut stuffing (see below)

Method

1. Stuff with chestnut stuffing.
2. Smear the turkey with butter and pin the greaseproof paper over the breast.
3. Roast for the time stated on the packaging; for the last 30 minutes, remove the paper and let the skin brown.

Chestnut Stuffing

1 can of chestnuts, chopped finely (or you could get fresh chestnuts: boil them until tender and then shell)

125 g bacon

2 tbsp chopped parsley

1 sprig marjoram

1 sprig thyme

¼ tsp mace

½ tsp nutmeg

Salt and pepper

Method

1. Chop the chestnuts and place them into a bowl. Then add the minced bacon and the rest of the ingredients and work well into a paste. Use this to stuff your Christmas turkey.

Bread Sauce

100 g fine white breadcrumbs

Salt and pepper

50 g butter

1 onion chopped finely

300 ml milk

2 tbsp cream

Method

1. Add the milk, butter, onions and breadcrumbs to a pan.
2. Heat gently until the onions are cooked and the butter has melted.
3. Add the cream and the seasoning to taste, and keep hot until served.

Sausage Shapes to go with the Turkey Dinner

The vegetables to go with this dish seemed, in Hanna Glasse's cookbook, to be anything you wanted, but she did have a recipe for parboiling potatoes, putting them in a pan of hot dripping and shaking the pan until brown. Not much different to what we do today, only we all seem to use tinned goose fat instead of dripping these days.

500 g lean pork
500 g beef suet
1 tsp allspice
1 tsp black pepper
½ tsp nutmeg
1 tsp salt

1 tsp fresh thyme, chopped

1 tsp, fresh marjoram, chopped

2 tsp fresh parsley, chopped

Method

1. Mince the pork in a food processor or a hand mincer.
2. Add the rest of the ingredients until it is nicely bound together (it should look like sausage meat).
3. Dust a board with flour and take pieces of the mixture, rolling them into long sausage shapes.
4. Grease an oven tray and arrange the sausages in shapes e.g. O, S, C and X.
5. Bake in a moderate oven for 30 minutes.
6. Arrange the sausage shapes on a platter decorated with fresh parsley and thyme, and serve with the Christmas turkey.

Eighteenth-Century North of England Festive Pie

This is a good recipe for a Boxing Day lunch with some pickle, but you will need a lot of guests to be serving a pie this size!

1 goose

1 partridge

1 pigeon

1 turkey

2 tsp mace

2 tsp black pepper

2 tsp nutmeg

½ tsp ground cloves

1 tsp salt

250 g butter

Hot water pastry

Method

1. Ask your butcher to bone all the birds for you.
2. Dust the smallest bird – the pigeon – in the spices and stuff it into the partridge.
3. Dust the partridge and stuff it into the goose.
4. Do the same with the goose and stuff it into the turkey.
5. Place this huge bird into a pre-shaped hot water crust pastry base, covered on top with slices of butter.
6. Pack around the bird some whole onions, parsnips and large chunks of turnip, also covered with the spice mixture and the butter.
7. Put the lid on top and bake for 4 hours in a moderate oven.
8. Take out of the oven and cut away the pastry lid. Lift the bird onto a platter and arrange it on top of the vegetables.
9. The pastry should be cut into pieces and put on a side plate to be eaten with the meal.

Duke of Buckingham's Pudding with Sherry Sauce

450 g suet

125 g big raisins chopped

2 eggs

1 tsp nutmeg

1 tsp ginger

125 g flour

50 g sugar

Sauce

75 g melted butter

3 tbsp sherry

3 tbsp sugar

Method

1. Mix all the pudding ingredients together in a bowl.
2. Dampen a large pudding cloth and flour it well all over.
3. Pour the mixture into the middle of the cloth and tie tightly.
4. Drop into a pan of boiling water and simmer for 3 hours.
5. Combine the sauce ingredients and pour over the pudding in dishes.

Christmas Cake with Icing

Here is very large cake from Hanna Glasse's cookbook.

2 kg flour	
3½ kg currants	
1½ kg butter	
1 kg almonds	
1 glass of sherry	
24 eggs	
1½ kg sugar	
1 tbsp mace powder	
1 tbsp cinnamon	
½ tbsp cloves	
1 tbsp nutmeg	
½ tsp ginger	
300 ml brandy	
2 oranges	
2 lemons	

Method

1. Cream the butter and sugar together. Add the eggs one at a time, with a spoonful of the flour with the spices sifted into it.
2. Add the brandy and mix in the fruit and nuts.
3. Add the rind and juice of the oranges and lemons and mix well.
4. Put in a large round cake tin and bake for 4 hours.

Icing to Ice a Great Cake

These are Hanna's words, not mine!

24 egg whites

450 g icing sugar

Method

1. The recipe calls for beating the egg whites and sugar for 4 hours – this must be a misprint, surely!
2. Then, with a bunch of feathers, spread the icing over the cake and put it back into a cool oven until the icing has dried. Be careful not to let it go brown.

Mincemeat

It is fascinating to learn that the Georgians made the sweet mincemeat that we know today, only they put it into pies between layers of meat.

1½ kg suet

1 kg raisins

1 kg currants

50 eating apples, peeled, cored and chopped finely

225 g sugar

1 tbsp mace

1 tbsp cloves

1 tbsp nutmeg

300 ml brandy

300 ml sherry

Method

1. Chop everything finely and mix it all together. Store in pots until needed.

Mince Pie

Pastry for a large dish

600 g mincemeat (see above)

300 g minced cold roast beef or tongue (or both mixed together)

2 oranges peeled with a knife and sliced thinly

Juice of 2 oranges

Method

1. Line a pie dish with pastry.
2. Put a thin layer of meat at the base, followed by a layer of orange slices, cut very thinly.
3. Top this with a layer of mincemeat.
4. Repeat the layers, finishing with the juice of the orange. Place the pie crust on top.
5. Bake in a moderate oven for 40 minutes until the pastry is nicely crisp. Eat in slices when cold.

Floating Islands

'A pretty dish for the middle of a table to be surrounded with candles.'

1 litre double cream	
150 ml sherry	
Peel of 3 lemons	
125 g icing sugar	
3 French rolls	
Various coloured jellies	
Jellied sweets	

Method

1. Put the lemon peel and sugar into the cream and leave for an hour to infuse. Then strain.
2. Add the sherry and beat it well until you have a thick foam on top.
3. Ladle the foam off and put it to one side.
4. Pour the cream onto a large platter.

5. Slice the rolls very thinly and gently place them on the cream, ensuring they are spread out.
6. Spread some jelly onto the roll slices and top with more slices of roll.
7. Repeat this, finishing with a slice of roll.
8. Beat the foam again to make it thick. Drop spoonfuls of the mixture on top of the floating rolls in the pool of cream.
9. Spread sweetmeats around the rim of the platter and surround it with candles. Use it as a centrepiece for your table.

The Victorians

The Victorians

IN THE EARLY PART of the nineteenth century, most people in the countryside and small towns of Britain ate the food they produced locally. Not until the railway network was built in the mid-nineteenth century did different delicacies sit on the tables of the masses. Simple things we all take for granted, like fresh milk every morning, was only brought about by the new railway distribution systems. Also thanks to the railway systems could fresh sea fish be taken inland each day, and in 1875 the new Billingsgate fish market was built in London as a distribution centre. It was a very grand building for the time and resembled a French château, or one of the famous spa hotels in Scotland. The palatial grandeur of the interior was almost created architecturally to resemble a church, so that homage could be paid to the humble fish.

By the 1860s, new roller mills produced white flour free of wheat germ to make cheap bread for the poorer classes to eat. How ironic that, in wanting to emulate the fine white bread of the gentry, they were in fact doing themselves out of the wholesomeness of the bread that they had always eaten in the past. Tinned foods were also developed as a way of bringing cheap products from the empire into the country, but at first they were only a curiosity among members of the rich households who could pay for them – odd, really, when you consider that they had more than enough fresh meat without needing poor-quality, canned Australian substitutes.

Chocolate was reinvented too, from a luxury drink into the solid bar for the mass market to delight in. It was in Switzerland that the Nestlé family developed the first milk chocolate. Strangely enough, the popularity of chocolate was promoted by the Quakers, who wanted to give the poor a cheap alternative drink to alcohol. The Fry family of York and the Cadbury family of Bourneville combined, doing God's work while making a nice profit for themselves at the same time. But to be fair, they did improve the lives of those that worked in their factories immensely, providing them with good housing, schools and health care. The chocolate bar as we know it today was not on the shelves of the sweet shops until 1847, when Fry's produced one cheap enough for the mass market.

Technological innovations in the average kitchen did not really take off until the 1880s, when gas works were built, not only to light the people's streets and homes, but also to fuel their gas cookers. It was an age of so much change – milled flour, baking powder to make lighter cakes and easily used ovens in most homes – that it truly fired the imaginations of the Victorian cooks.

Penny-in-the-slot gas meters made it possible for even the poorest people to use these facilities too. So suddenly there was a huge market for pans, biscuit cutters, ladles, jelly moulds and pie tins to accommodate this new culinary revolution. Towards the end of the century, these items began to be made out of enamel and aluminium, and by the end of the nineteenth century, the refrigerator could be seen in many middle-class homes. It was no longer just the nobility who could enjoy sorbets and ice creams.

Important though this new kitchen equipment was, nothing changed the British diet so much as the food that poured into every port from the far reaches of the British Empire. The Victorian middle classes virtually had the world on their plates as more and more exotic food combinations became a normal part of their diet. The word 'curry', originally 'Kari', was a Tamil word for spiced food that has now become a part of the British vocabulary. This category of Victorian food is so important that I have given it its own section. But first of all, I will introduce you to some of their recipes without spices.

Prince of Wales Soup

This soup was apparently invented by a philanthropic friend of Mrs Beeton's editor. It was used to feed the poor in a large village to celebrate the coming of age of the Prince of Wales. When I heard of this account, I thought the soup would be a bit special for such an occasion, but as you can see, it is seriously frugal. I suppose the poor at the time would have been grateful for any hot food, but I think she could have put a bit of meat into it!

12 turnips

2 tbsp sugar

2 tbsp strong veal stock

Salt and pepper to taste

2 quarts beef stock

1 loaf of bread

Method

1. Peel the turnips and chop into small pieces.
2. Put them in the stock and simmer gently until tender.
3. Add the veal stock and other ingredients.
4. Cut the loaf into slices and then cut each slice into small circles. Gently drop the circles into the tureen and ladle the soup over them. Care has to be taken not to put the soup in too quickly, or the bread circles would crumple and the appearance of the soup would be spoiled.

Brillat Savarin's Fondue

8 eggs
120 g Gruyere cheese
80 g butter
Salt and pepper to taste
Bread cubes
1 bottle burgundy

Method

1. Beat the eggs well in a bowl and add the grated cheese and butter cut into small pieces.
2. Stir the mixture together. Then, set the bowl into a pan of water over the heat until the cheese and butter melts. It should be nice and thick.
3. Then add the seasoning to taste and pour into a sliver or metal dish.
4. Serve immediately with bread cubes for dunking and a glass of burgundy wine.

Macaroni Cheese

225 g macaroni

100 g butter

175 g of Parmesan or
Cheshire cheese

600 ml milk

1 litre water

75 g fine breadcrumbs

Salt and pepper to taste

Method

1. Bring the milk, water and salt to the boil and drop
   in the macaroni. Boil until tender.
2. Drain the macaroni and put it in a deep dish.
3. Reserve some cheese for the top and add the rest
   to the macaroni with most of the butter. Stir well
   and season with pepper.
4. Mix the remaining cheese with the breadcrumbs
   and sprinkle over the macaroni.

5. Melt the remaining butter and pour it over the breadcrumbs and cheese.
6. Brown the top under a hot grill and serve immediately.

Toasted Cheese Sandwich

Slices of brown bread and
butter

½ inch thick slices of cheese,
either Cheddar or Cheshire

Method

1. Make the sandwiches with the thick slices of cheese
   and put them on an oven tray.
2. Bake in a hot oven for 10 minutes until the bread it
   toasted.
3. Serve hot on a napkin and eat quickly.

Bubble and Squeak

This is the original bubble and squeak recipe that does not include potatoes. They were added during the Second World War to make the greens go a bit farther.

A few slices of cold roast beef

50 g butter

1 large onion, sliced

450 g cooked greens, either cabbage or Brussels sprouts

Salt and pepper to taste

Method

1. Fry the slices of meat in the butter, gently taking care not to dry them out.
2. Lay them on a dish and keep hot.

3. Fry the chopped cooked greens with the onions in a pan with the butter until the onion is soft. Season with salt and pepper.
4. Put on top of the meat and serve at once.

Lark Pie

I put this recipe in just as a curiosity. Please don't kill any larks to try it for yourself! The Victorians clearly did not have much of a love for birdsong. You could replace the larks with quail or small pigeons if you wanted to try it.

2 slices of beef (rump steak, beaten well until it is thin)
2 slices of bacon (gammon steak, also beaten until thin)
9 larks (pigeon or quail)
75 g flour
250 g breadcrumbs
Peel of 1 lemon
1 tsp chopped parsley
1 egg
Salt and pepper to taste

2 chopped shallots

300 ml stock

Puff pastry

Method

1. Make the stuffing with breadcrumbs, lemon peel, parsley, and the egg.
2. Stuff the birds with it and roll them in flour.
3. In a deep dish, lay the slices of beef and bacon and put the birds on top of them.
4. Sprinkle with salt and pepper, and add more parsley and chopped shallot.
5. Pour the stock over the birds and then put the puff pastry crust on top.
6. Bake in a moderate oven for 1 hour. During that time, take the pie out and shake it a few times to help make the gravy.
7. Serve very hot – and mind the bones!

Oyster Stew

Oysters were a very cheap food in Victorian times, and were eaten by everyone – perhaps this is why they are so scarce today.

12 plump oysters
150 ml cream
¼ tsp mace
¼ tsp cayenne
Salt
50 g butter
1 tsp flour
A handful of small cubes of fried bread

Method

1. Wash the oysters well and strain the liquor from the shells. Put in a pan with the oysters and heat slowly.
2. When they just begin to simmer, take the oysters out and take off their beards.
3. Add to the pan the cream and spices, and when it boils add the butter mixed with the flour. Stir continuously until it is smooth.
4. Then put in the oysters and keep them on a low heat until they heat through in the hot sauce.
5. Serve at once sprinkled with the fried bread cubes or sippets, as they were called.

Salmon Pudding

450 g salmon

225 g breadcrumbs

1 tsp anchovy essence

150 ml cream

4 eggs

Salt and cayenne pepper

Method

1. Poach salmon in water for 20 minutes.
2. Fork the cooked salmon, making sure there are no bones or skin on it.
3. Mix well with the breadcrumbs and add the anchovy essence, cream and cayenne.
4. Beat the eggs and add them to the mixture.
5. Press the mixture into an ovenproof dish that has been well buttered and bake for 1 hour in a moderate oven.
6. Serve hot or cold with a salad.

Boiled Beef and Carrots

A scaled-down version of a Mrs Beeton recipe.

2 kg joint of beef silverside	
2 tbsp salt	
Water	
1 kg whole carrots	

Method

1. Cover the meat in salt and leave in the fridge for at least 2 days. Then wash off the salt.
2. Get a big pan of water boiling and put the beef in it. Then reduce it to a simmer and cook for at least 3 hours, removing the scum as you cook it.
3. During the last 40 minutes, add 1 kg of peeled whole carrots.

4. Take the beef out of the stock – which can be made into pea soup – and slice the ends off the joint as they will be tough and not pleasant to look at.
5. Put the beef on a large platter surrounded by the whole cooked carrots.

Breast of Lamb with Peas

1 breast of lamb

4 slices of bacon, thick cut

300 ml stock

1 lemon

A bunch each of mint and
parsley

450 g green peas

Method

1. Remove the skin from the breast of lamb and put it in a saucepan of boiling water. Simmer for 5 minutes, and then take it out and put it in cold water.
2. Line the bottom of a casserole dish with the bacon and put the lamb on top.
3. Peel the lemon with a knife and slice it thinly. Lay it over the lamb.

4. Cover with more slices of bacon.
5. Add the stock, onion and roughly chopped herbs and simmer until tender – about 1 hour.
6. Cook the peas, drain, and put them in a large dish. Lay the bacon and lamb on top and then serve.

Beef Stew à la Mode

1½ kg stewing beef	
50 g beef dripping	
1 large onion, sliced finely	
50 g flour (with 1 tsp salt in it)	
2 litres boiling water	
12 berries of allspice	
2 bay leaves	
½ tsp whole pepper	
Salt to taste	

Method

1. Cut the beef into small pieces and roll in the flour.
2. Put the dripping in a pan and fry the onions in it. When brown, take the onions out.
3. Add the beef and brown it all over.
4. Put into a large pan with the onions pour the water over it and add the rest of the ingredients. Cover the pan and simmer gently for 3 hours.

Beef à la Mode

3½ kg beef

575 g lard

2 thick slices of fat bacon

300 ml vinegar

½ tsp back pepper

1 tsp allspice

1 tsp ground cloves

A bunch of fresh savoury, parsley and thyme (mixed)

3 onions

2 large carrots

1 turnip

1 head of celery

900 ml water

150 ml port

Method

1. Fry the sliced onion in the lard until pale brown.
2. Cut up the other vegetables into small pieces.

3. Chop the herbs finely and mix with the spice.
4. Dip the bacon in the vinegar and then rub into it the herb and spice mix.
5. Lay the bacon on the beef, then roll it up and tie it tightly with string. Rub the rest of the herb and spice mix over it.
6. Put the vegetables, vinegar and water into a pan just a little bigger than the beef joint. Then put the beef in and simmer gently for 5 hours.
7. When it is tender, take the beef out and cut off the string, skimming off any fat from the stock. Add the port wine and let it come to the boil. Then pour this with the vegetables over the beef and serve at once with boiled mashed potatoes.

Bermuda Witches

1 Madeira cake or a plain
butter cake

150 g guava jelly

150 g finely grated fresh
coconut (or desiccated
coconut that has been left
in boiling water for 2 hours
and drained)

Method

1. Cut the brown edges off the cake and slice it
   horizontally.
2. Spread one half with the Guava jelly and sprinkle
   the coconut on top. Then put the other slice on
   top.
3. Cut into finger-sized pieces and lay in a sloping
   fashion on a white napkin on a plate. Dust with
   sugar and garnish with myrtle sprigs or bay leaves
   between the slices.

Victoria Sandwich

I had to put in Mrs Beeton's Victoria sandwich recipe, even though it is still seen in most cookbooks today. Interestingly, it was originally made in a rectangular cake tin and cut into fingers, rather than made in the round sandwich tins that we are used to today.

4 eggs and their weight in caster sugar, butter and flour

2 pinches of salt

450 g jam or marmalade

Method

1. Beat the butter and the sugar together until it becomes pale.
2. Add the eggs one at a time and beat well.
3. Fold in the flour using a metal spoon.
4. Butter a Swiss roll tin and pour the cake mix into it.
5. Bake in a hot oven for 20 minutes until it is firm and golden brown.
6. When cool, cut it into half and spread the jam or marmalade on one half and put the other half on top and dust with icing sugar.
7. Cut into long, finger-shaped pieces and arrange on a glass plate in a crisscross fashion.

Manchester Pudding

75 g breadcrumbs	
300 ml milk	
1 strip of lemon peel	
4 eggs	
50 g butter	
50 g sugar	
Puff pastry	
1 jar of jam	
1 tbsp brandy	

Method

1. Flavour the milk with the lemon peel by infusing it in the cold milk for 30 minutes.
2. Strain and pour it into the breadcrumbs and put it in a pan. Boil for 2–3 minutes.
3. Add the 4 egg yolks, 2 egg whites, butter, sugar and brandy and stir well together.

4. Line a pie dish with puff pastry and cover it with a thick layer of jam.
5. When the other mixture is cold, pour it over the jam and bake in the oven for 1 hour.
6. Serve cold with a little sifted icing sugar on it.

Chantilly Basket

1 mould (could be a bowl or a cone-shaped dish)	
1 packet of small round macaroons	
1 packet of barley sugar sweets	
300 ml double cream	
50 g icing sugar	
450 g strawberries or raspberries	

Method

1. Crush the barley sugar sweets and very slowly melt them in a pan over a heat.
2. Carefully dip the edges of the macaroons into the melted barley sugar and glue them together inside your mould. This takes some time, as you need to make sure that they have enough of the toffee to glue them well together.

3. Leave it to set for 2 hours and take your macaroon basket out of your mould.
4. Whip the cream with the sugar, then chop half the strawberries/raspberries and mix with the cream.
5. Just before you serve, pile the strawberry cream into your basket and decorate with whole strawberries on the top. Dust with icing sugar and serve, cutting into the basket for each portion.

Oranges Filled with Jelly

4 very large oranges

Gelatine to make 600 ml of jelly

Red food colouring

Method

1. Cut a small hole in the top of the oranges and carefully scoop out the contents.
2. Make a jelly out of the squeezed juice of the oranges with added sugar and put red food colouring in half of it.
3. Alternately spoon layers of orange jelly and red coloured jelly into the oranges, leaving it to set between layers. If the jellies start to set, warm them in a bowl of hot water again.
4. When they are filled to the top, leave them overnight to set really well.
5. Cut the oranges into quarters, revealing their striped jelly contents and arrange them on a dish with sprigs of myrtle between them.

Apples in Red Jelly

6 apples

12 cloves

100 g sugar

1 lemon

600 ml water

1 tbsp gelatine

Red food colouring
(cochineal if you can get it)

Method

1. Peel the apples and core them. Add two cloves to the hole and as much icing sugar as it will hold.
2. Put them in a large pie dish without letting them touch each other and add the rest of the sugar, the juice of the lemon and the water. Bake in an oven until they are cooked, but do not overcooked them or they will lose their shape.
3. Carefully place the apples in a glass dish, again without letting them touch each other.

4. Strain the liquor the apples have been cooked in and add the rind of the lemon and the gelatine (already dissolved in cold water). Put them in a pan with more sugar if desired and more cloves if necessary. Boil until quite clear, and then add a few drops of red colouring and strain.
5. When cooler, pour around the apples in the glass bowl, leaving the tops of the apples exposed. When cold, garnish the tops of the apple cores with brightly coloured lemon marmalade.

Open Jelly with Whipped Cream

To make this you will need a circular mould or cake tin with a hole in the centre. The Victorians had so many different jelly moulds that there must have been a rather nice income for those companies involved in producing them! No doubt the rich would constantly seek out new sizes and shapes for their many dinner parties.

1½ packets of jelly, preferably dark in colour

300 ml cream

1 glass sherry

Sugar to taste

Method

1. Make the jelly and fill your circular mould, previously soaked in cold water for 1 hour.
2. When set, turn the jelly out onto a dish.
3. Whip the cream with a little sugar and the sherry, and pile into the middle of the jelly.
4. Shape the cream to a conical point and dust with icing sugar on the very top so that it looks like a snow-capped mountain.

Victorian Curries

SOME OF THE PRODUCTS that many of us use today originally came from the colonies. One example, of which you may not be aware, is Worcestershire sauce. A Lord Sandys, who was an aristocrat from Worcestershire, apparently came across the recipe when he was the governor of Bengal. In 1835 he is said to have asked two chemists – John Lea and William Perrins – to make some for him from the recipe. This they did, making a jar or two extra for themselves at the same time. But on tasting it, they did not like it at all and put it on a shelf in their cellar and forgot about it. Quite some time later, they found the jars and tasted it again, finding that, after it had matured, it made a delicious sauce. To this day, the exact ingredients are a secret of the Lea and Perrins factory.

One of the most common condiments on any café table today is HP sauce, which was invented to accommodate this new taste for spicy food. A man called Frederick Gibson Garton, who was a grocer from Nottingham, invented the recipe, and because it became popular in one of the restaurants of the Houses of Parliament, he gave it the name HP. Unfortunately his enterprise fell on hard times and he had to sell his recipe and the HP brand to a man called Edwin Samson Moore, the founder of the Midlands Vinegar Company (and the forerunner of HP Foods Corporation).

Tomatoes originally imported into Britain in the Elizabethan period suddenly became popular as a basic ingredient for the sauces and chutneys used to accompany curries. When we think of the chutney served with our ploughman's lunch at the pub, it seems so very British, and yet it comes directly from the days of the Raj.

One might think that all the curried foods brought to Britain came from the Indian continent alone, but this is not entirely true. There were other, subtler, secondary influences on the spicy dishes that landed on British tables during the Victorian period. This came about when the British sent labourers from India to work in their new plantations in other far-flung parts of the world. They went to Kenya, Uganda, South Africa, Ceylon, the West Indies, Fiji and Australia, to name but a few. Those Indian labourers took their Indian cuisine with them, and adapted it to the local foods where they now lived. Places like South Africa, for instance, had the perfect climate to produce many lucrative crops, including arrowroot, pineapples, bananas, coffee, etc.

Babotie, a curried minced meat dish, was brought to British tables from the Malaysian migrant workers in Cape Town. The spicy scotch bonnet chilli from Trinidad was added to West Indian curries to give them their fire. The Victorians also added completely alien vegetables to the traditional Indian foods, such as tomatoes, corn, potatoes and kidney beans. When we think of authentic curries at a takeaway, most people would assume a dry potato curry was typically Indian, but, of course, this was a Victorian British invention.

It is believed that the first Indian restaurant in Britain was called The Hindustanee Coffee House in London in 1809. Its owner, Dean Mahomed, had been a cook for a British officer in India and had returned to Britain with the officer when he retired. He knew just how the British liked their curries – a more general version of his country's regional cuisines. These curries were adapted to suit all British palates, from the very spicy to the very mild. Unfortunately, he was a little ahead of his time and his restaurant closed just three years later. It was not until the later Victorian period, with its vast movement of men and women to and from India and the colonies, that the British population really acquired a taste for a good curry. The traditional food of Britain seemed bland and tasteless in comparison to the intricately spiced dishes that they had become so used to. On news of returning home, those Brits would have had their cooks devise curry powder combinations and pastes, so that they could replicate the dishes they knew and loved. Of course, when Queen Victoria herself had Indian cooks in the palace to cook authentic dishes at palace functions, it then became a must have ingredient for all those who aspired to be associated with the nobility.

Korma – one of our favourite curries – originated in the Islamic courts of the moguls in the eleventh century. In India, Pakistan and Bangladesh, the word *korma* means a rich banquet dish, and as turmeric is never used in a korma, it keeps its pale, thick, creamy, rich look. The Malaysian kormas are slightly different to the Indian ones, as they have coconut milk in them. This is the korma I like, with its thick coconut sauce and slight sweetness. Korma was the curry of choice for those in Britain that liked the taste of spice, but not the heat of it. In contrast to the korma was of course the madras curry, or the vindaloo that had its origins in Portuguese-occupied Goa. It was generally made of pork and the name comes from the

Portuguese words for wine (*vinho*) and *alhos* (garlic). It was probably a simple stew originally, but has now acquired its world famous reputation for being one of the hottest curries you can eat. It is still almost a rite of passage for young men on their first group trips to curry houses in Britain.

One of the most popular Anglo-Indian tastes was the dish of curried eggs. The British were traditionally used to having eggs for breakfast, but while in the tropics they also enjoyed eating curries for breakfast, and so it seems that they combined the two, and curried eggs were born. So popular was this dish that it was very often eaten for lunch as well as breakfast.

Mrs Beeton's Curry Powder

Mrs Beeton said that it was just as good to buy curry powder, and was usually cheaper than making it.

125 g coriander seeds

125 g turmeric

50 g cinnamon

2 tsp cayenne

25 g mustard seed

25 g ground ginger

1 tbsp allspice

50 g fenugreek seed

Method

1. Grind all the above in a mortar and store in an airtight tin.

Mr Arnott's Currie Powder

Eliza Acton's book included this recipe.

225 g turmeric
125 g coriander seed
125 g cumin seed
125 g fenugreek seed
1 tbsp cayenne pepper

Method

1. Grind all the ingredients in a mortar, as with the recipe above, and store in an airtight container.

Mr Arnott's Currie

1 cabbage heart (take all the
green leaves off a cabbage
until you just have the pale
ones)

2 eating apples

Juice of 1 lemon

½ tsp pepper

1 tbsp curry powder

6 onions

A whole head of garlic

50 g butter

2 tbsp flour

600 ml beef gravy or rich
stock made with stock cubes

Cayenne pepper to taste

450 g cooked chicken or
mutton or rabbit or lobster
or the remains of yesterday's
calf's head roast

Method

1. Chop the cabbage heart finely and slice the peeled, cored apples thinly.
2. In a bowl, mix together the cabbage, apples, lemon juice, pepper and curry powder.
3. Fry the sliced onions in the butter until brown, and then add the minced garlic. Add the flour and cook for 1 minute.
3. Add the stock and the rest of the ingredients and bring to the boil, simmering for 30 minutes.
4. Add the meat of your choice and heat through, adding more cayenne if it is not hot enough.
5. Serve with plain boiled rice.

Curried Beef

225 g lean cold roast beef,
cut into cubes

75 g butter

2 onions

300 ml beer

1 dessertspoonful of curry
powder

Method

1. Fry the onion in the butter until light brown, and then add the rest of the ingredients. Simmer for 10 minutes.
2. It should be a thick curry, but if it is too dry, add a little more beer or water.
3. Serve in the middle of a bed of boiled rice.

Curried Eggs

8 hard-boiled eggs

1 large onion

1 tbsp flour

1 tbsp curry powder

300 ml chicken stock

Juice of 1 lemon

1 eating apple, peeled, cored
and grated

3 tbsp chutney

50 g butter

Method

1. Fry the onion until golden brown in the butter.
2. Add the curry powder and cook for 1 minute.
3. Add the flour and cook for another minute.
4. Pour in the stock and bring to the boil, stirring all
   the time to thicken.

5. Add the whole peeled eggs, grated apple and chutney.
6. Simmer for 30 minutes for the curry sauce to impregnate the whites of the eggs.
7. Serve with plain boiled rice.

Mutton Curry

From London's Oriental Club in the 1860s.

75 g butter	
2 large onions	
2 tbsp curry powder	
1 tbsp curry paste	
1 kg mutton	
1 tsp salt	

Method

1. Cook the onions in the butter until lightly browned.
2. Add the curry powder and paste to the pan and cook for 1 minute, stirring all the time.
3. Add the cubed mutton and cook until the meat is brown.

4. Pour in 500 ml water or enough to cover it well and add the salt.
5. Bring the water to the boil and, if you have one, put it in a slow cooker for 5 hours. Alternatively, place in a sealed pot on a low oven shelf for 3 hours.

Kedgeree

This dish originally came from Bombay, and was called 'Khichri', consisting of rice, lentils, hard-boiled eggs and scattered with raisins; the fish was served separately. It was adapted into many variations of the recipe below, and was brought back from India to become a favourite breakfast dish during the Victorian period.

A large dish of kedgeree would be kept warm with a candle under it on the sideboard of the average Victorian family, along with bacon, eggs and devilled kidneys.

150 g smoked haddock

225 g cooked rice

25 g butter

1 tsp mustard

2 hard-boiled eggs

1 tbsp parsley, chopped

1 tsp salt

¼ tsp cayenne pepper

1 onion

Method

1. Chop the onion finely and fry until golden in the butter.
2. Mix in the pre-cooked and pre-boned flaked fish, rice, salt and cayenne pepper.
3. Chop the boiled eggs roughly and mix in with the parsley. Serve at once.

Curried Cod

This is a lovely, creamy curry. Miss out the cayenne and it is a perfect dish for those who prefer their curry a little milder.

450 g cod fillet (cooked, flaked and boned)
75 g butter
1 onion, sliced
300 ml chicken stock
1 tbsp flour
1 tbsp curry powder
150 ml cream
1 tsp salt
¼ tsp cayenne

Method

1. Fry the onions in the butter until brown and add the flaked fish.
2. Add the flour and curry powder and cook for 1 minute. Then gradually stir in the stock.
3. Simmer for 10 minutes and then stir in the cream, seasoning and cayenne.
4. Heat through and serve at once.

Curried Chicken

225 g cooked chicken (or
more if you have it)

2 large onions

Garlic (optional)

1 apple

50 g butter

1 tbsp curry powder

1 tsp flour

300 ml left over chicken
gravy

1 tbsp lemon juice

Method

1. Slice the onions and garlic (if desired) and peel, core and slice the apple. Fry in butter until tender.
2. Add the cooked chicken.
3. Add the flour and curry powder and cook for a further 3 minutes.
4. Gradually add the gravy and bring it to the boil.
5. Add the lemon juice and serve in a ring of cooked rice.

Mulligatawny Soup

This soup or stew can be traced to the beginnings of the East India Company in Madras. It was so widespread in popularity that Mrs Beeton had her own special recipe for it. Atkinson, a captain in the Engineers in 1854, wrote a poem about his trip to India in which he mentioned the soup:

First a sun, fierce and glaring, that scorches and bakes,
Palankeens, perspiration and worry,
Mosquitoes, thugs, cocoa-nuts, Brahmins, and snakes,
With elephants, tigers and Curry.

Then jungles, fakers, dancing girls, prickly heat,
Shawls, idols, durbars, brandy-pawny,
Rupees, clever jugglers, dust storms, slipper'd feet,
Rainy season and mulligatawny.

With Rajahs ... But stop, I must desist,
And let each one enjoy his opinions,
Whilst I who in what style Anglo-Indians exist,
In her Majesty's Eastern dominions.

It paints a vivid picture of the India he knew. A Palankeen was a closed litter carried by four servants, and Brandy-pawny is brandy and water. One thing it does show, though, was how much a part of their Indian life mulligatawny was. The name of this famous soup derives from the Tamil words *molegoo* (pepper) and *tunes* (water), meaning 'pepper water'. It was originally a vegetarian soup, but the British added meat and other ingredients to it to make a whole host of variations in India, Ceylon, and, of course, Britain.

1 litre chicken stock

250 g cooked chicken breast, finely chopped

200 g coconut cream

1 tsp cumin

1 tsp coriander

1 tsp chilli powder

1 small tin tomato puree

2 onions chopped

2 tablespoons chutney

3 cardamom pods

Salt and pepper

2 tbsp butter

Sprig of fresh coriander

Method

1. Fry the onion in the butter until soft.
2. Add the spices to the onions and cook for 5 minutes.
3. Add the other ingredients and bring to the boil.
4. Simmer for 30 minutes and serve sprinkled with chopped coriander leaves.

Coconut Soup

Here is another exotically inspired Victorian soup from Mrs Beeton.

100 g grated coconut

150 g rice flour

½ tsp mace

1 tsp salt

150 ml cream

2 quarts chicken stock

Cayenne to taste

Method

1. Grate the fresh coconut.
2. Add the coconut to the stock, mace and salt and simmer for 1 hour.
3. Strain and thicken with the rice flour and add the cream and cayenne to taste.

Tomato Sauce (for keeping)

To accompany the new fashion for curries, all kinds of catsups, sauces and chutneys were developed. The tomato that was introduced into Britain during Elizabethan times only really became popular during this period as a central ingredient in these essential curry accompaniments.

1 quart tomato pulp (this could be the pulp you buy in cartons or tins)
600 ml vinegar
1 tsp cayenne pepper
50 g shallots
6 cloves garlic
Salt to taste

Method

1. If using fresh tomatoes, bake them in a slow oven until tender and rub through a sieve or liquidise into a pulp.
2. Add the pulp to a large pan with the other ingredients and boil until the garlic and shallots are soft.
3. Take the garlic and shallots out and put them through a sieve. Then put them back into the pan with the other ingredients. This sauce is ready to use in one week and will keep for 2–3 years.

   NB. For a richer sauce, add 600 ml soy sauce and 600 ml of anchovy sauce to every 6 quarts and cook for another 20 minutes.

Mushroom Ketchup

1 kg mushrooms

375 g salt

For each litre of mushroom liquid add:

25 g pepper

1 tbsp allspice

1 tbsp ginger

2 blades of mace

Method

1. Put the mushrooms into a large jar and cover with salt and mix. Put a piece of greaseproof paper over the top and leave them overnight.
2. Strain and boil the liquid for 15 minutes.
3. For every quart of liquid, add the spices and boil for a further 15 minutes. Bottle and use to flavour sauce and curries.

Bengal Mango Chutney

This interesting recipe contains no mangoes, despite its name. Mrs Beeton also says that it was given to an English lady by a native who had lived in India for most of her adult life. Since her return to England, she had become quite celebrated amongst her friends for this excellent eastern relish. If you look at the ingredients, you will see it was incredibly hot too.

700 g moist brown sugar

350 g salt

100 g garlic

100 g onions

350 g fresh ginger (this is what it says in her book!)

100 g dried chillies

100 g mustard seeds

350 g raisins

2 quarts vinegar

30 large, unripe, sour apples

Method

1. Slowly dissolve the sugar into syrup with a few tablespoons of water.
2. In a mortar, pound the garlic, onions and ginger.
3. The mustard seed must be washed in cold vinegar and dried in the sun (why this has to be done, I can't imagine).
4. Peel the apples and core them, then slice and boil them in 1½ litres of the vinegar until soft. Let this go cold before doing anything else.
5. Put everything else into a large pan with the rest of the vinegar and mix very well.
6. Bottle in the usual way.

Indian Pickle

This is better known today as piccalilli. This is a very large batch, so scale it down unless you are planning to give it to friends.

4 quarts vinegar

6 cloves of garlic

12 shallots

2 sticks of sliced horseradish (or 2 tbsp horseradish sauce will do)

100 g bruised ginger

50 g black pepper whole

25 g pepper capsicum

25 g allspice

12 whole cloves

1 tsp cayenne pepper

50 g mustard seed

100 g English mustard (not powdered)

25 g turmeric
1 cabbage (white)
1 cauliflower
A bunch of radishes
250 g French beans
250 g cucumbers or gherkins fresh
250 g small pickling onions
100 g nasturtium seed pods (if you can't get these, large capers will do)
250 g green peppers

Method

1. Cut the cabbage into slices and the cauliflower into branches, and put in a large bowl. Sprinkle with salt and leave for two days.
2. Dry them and put them into a very large jar, with garlic, shallots, horseradish, ginger, pepper, allspice and cloves.
3. Boil enough vinegar to cover them and leave for two days.

4. Then add to the jar the rest of the vegetables to be pickled, making sure they are always covered with vinegar. Leave for two days.

5. Take out the vegetables and pack them into jars without the vinegar.

6. Put the vinegar in a pan and bring it to the boil. Add the cayenne, mustard seed, turmeric and mustard (all of which must have been mixed with a little cold vinegar first).

7. When the vinegar is boiling hot, pour it over the pickles in the jars.

NB. This pickle will keep for years and was a real favourite with cold meat.

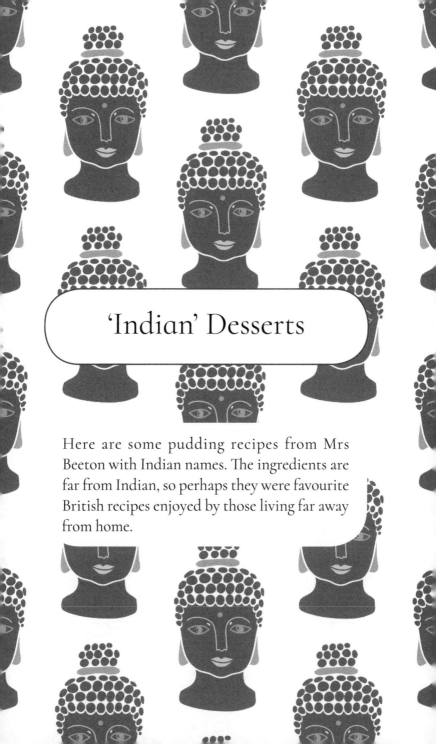

'Indian' Desserts

Here are some pudding recipes from Mrs Beeton with Indian names. The ingredients are far from Indian, so perhaps they were favourite British recipes enjoyed by those living far away from home.

Delhi Pudding

4 large apples

A little grated nutmeg

1 tsp minced lemon zest

2 tabs sugar

150 g currants

350 g suet crust pastry (half suet to flour with a pinch of salt)

Method

1. Peel, core and slice the apples and put them in a saucepan with the nutmeg, sugar and lemon peel.
2. Cook until soft and then leave to go cold.
3. Roll the suet crust pastry into a large rectangle.
4. Spread the apple mix over it and sprinkle with currants.
5. Roll it up and seal the edges with water.

6. Flour a large, damp pudding cloth with a generous amount of flour and put the pudding onto it. Tie it well.
7. Boil in a large pan for 2 hours and eat at once with custard.

Indian Fritters

3 tbsp flour

4 egg yolks

2 egg whites

Lard for frying

Jam for serving

Method

1. Put the flour into a bowl and add enough boiling water to make a stiff paste.
2. Leave it to cool and then break into it the egg yolks and the egg whites. Beat until smooth.
3. Have a pan of boiling lard or butter ready and drop spoonfuls of the batter into it. Cook until light brown. They should rise when they are cooked, like balls.
4. Serve immediately with a spoonful of jam on each fritter.

Indian Trifle

1 quart milk

Rind of a large lemon

Sugar to taste

5 heaped tbsp rice flour

25 g flaked almonds

300 ml custard

Method

1. Simmer the milk and lemon rind together for 5 minutes and stir in the rice flour (previously moistened with milk and enough sugar to sweeten it).
2. Boil and then simmer for 5 minutes, stirring all the time.
3. Take it away from the heat and cool. Then pour onto a broad, shallow glass dish.
4. Let it go completely cold and then cut star shapes carefully out of the rice pudding, filling in the holes with cold custard.

5. Decorate the custard with flaked almonds stuck in upright.
6. Decorate the rice with coloured pieces of jelly or preserved fruits.

Pineapple Fritters

Mrs Beeton says that this is a very elegant dish, and would have been cheap to make because of all the pineapples arriving on ships from the West Indies.

1 small pineapple

1 small wineglass of brandy or liqueur

50 g icing sugar

300 ml batter (made with 300 ml milk, 1 egg and 100 g flour)

Method

1. Pare the pineapples and core and slice thinly.
2. Soak these in the liqueur or brandy and sugar for 4 hours.
3. Make the batter and dip the slices into it. Fry them in boiling lard for 5 minutes until they are brown on both sides.
4. Place onto a white doyley and sift icing sugar over the top. Serve immediately.

Victorian Christmas

Victorian Christmas

Roast Goose

5 kg goose

Stuffing

3 onions

4 large cooking apples

2 tbsp sage leaves

½ tsp pepper

½ tsp salt

2 tbsp melted butter

Gravy

500 ml stock (giblets and
wing tips of goose boiled
in water for 1 hour to make
stock)

1 onion

2 carrots

2 tbsp goose fat

1 bay leaf

3 sprigs parsley

1 sprig thyme

1 sprig marjoram

Salt and pepper to taste

Method

1. Rub the outside of the goose and inside the cavity with salt.
2. Chop the onions for the stuffing and fry with the butter, salt, pepper and sage until transparent.
3. When cooked, chop the apple and add this to the mixture. Then stuff the bird with it.
4. Put the bird on a wire rack in a roasting tin and bake in a hot oven for 20 minutes. Then reduce the heat and cook for 20 minutes per 500 g. Halfway though the cooking time, turn the goose over and drain the fat from beneath the rack.
5. While the goose is roasting, make the gravy by adding some goose fat to a pan along with the onion and carrots.
6. Cook until browned, and then add the stock and seasoning. Simmer for 1 hour.

Roast Turkey and Sausage Meat Stuffing

The Victorians really invented the roast turkey Christmas dinner we eat today, including the stuffing, bread sauce, sausages, thick gravy and all the usual vegetables.

7 kg turkey
Flour for dusting
225 g melted butter
Greaseproof paper
Salt

Stuffing
175 g lean pork
175 g fat pork
50 g breadcrumbs
1 tbsp chopped sage
½ tsp mace, powdered

1 tsp salt

¼ tsp pepper

1 egg

Method

1. Make the stuffing by chopping the pork meats finely and mix well with the other ingredients. Stuff the bird with the stuffing and spread the breast with butter.
2. Roast the turkey for the time stated on the packaging, but instead of covering it in foil, cover it in buttered greaseproof paper and baste with the juices every half an hour.
3. For the last 15 minutes, take off the paper and dust with seasoned flour and ladle over the melted butter. This will crisp up the skin nicely.
4. Serve with bread sauce, sausages and all the trimmings.

Brawn

An Elizabethan recipe, brawn was just as popular in Victorian households.

1 pig's head, cut into halves	
300 g salt	
8 onions	
2 tbsp dried sage	
1 tbsp peppercorns	
½ tsp pepper ground	

Method

1. Rub the salt all over the halved pig's head and put in a pan. Leave for 2–3 days.
2. Take the brains out and poach them in water for about 30 minutes (these would disintegrate if cooked for longer).

3. Wash all the pieces well with cold water and put in a large pan, just covering them with water. Add the peppercorns and simmer for 2–3 hours until the meat is coming off the bones.
3. Lift the pieces onto a tray and leave the liquor to cool.
4. Take all the meat off the bones and mince it with a fork. Add the sage, chopped onion and pepper and salt to taste (some liked to keep the eyes and brains whole as a centrepiece, but that is up to you. If you don't want to do this, just mince the eyes along with the meat and the poached brain).
5. Remove the fat from the surface of the liquor and strain the liquor through a thick cloth.
6. Return 4 litres of this liquor to the cleaned pan and add the meat, onion and sage.
7. Simmer for 15 minutes, stirring frequently.
8. Have ready about a dozen pie dishes and basins and pour the mixture into them, leaving it to go cold.
9. When it is turned out, it is covered by a lovely glossy jelly and tastes delicious with applesauce and bread.

Mrs Beeton's Unrivalled Christmas Pudding

This is enough to make at least four big puddings, so you can either divide the quantities or make the entire batch and give them as Christmas presents.

675 g muscatel raisins

675 g currants

450 g sultanas

1 kg soft brown sugar

1 kg breadcrumbs

16 eggs

1 kg suet

175 g candied peel

The rind of 2 lemons

25 g nutmeg

25 g cinnamon

25 g ground almonds

150 ml brandy

Method

1. Mix all the dry ingredients together.
2. Beat the eggs together and add the brandy.
3. Mix the remainder of the ingredients with the eggs.
4. If you are going to make a huge pudding for a lot of people, dampen a large pudding cloth and butter and flour it very well. Put the pudding mix onto it and tie it tightly, boiling for 6–8 hours. If you are going to divide it into four, use either four pudding cloths for a traditional round pudding or greased and floured pudding basins. These will still need at least 3 hours' cooking time.
5. Cover with a fresh cloth when cold and store until Christmas Day.
6. Place in a fresh, dampened and floured cloth and boil for another 3 hours for the big pudding, and another hour for the smaller ones.

Plum Pudding Sauce

1 wineglass of brandy

50 g butter

1 glass Madeira

50 g icing sugar to taste

Method

1. Put the sugar and butter along with a little of the brandy into a basin and stand in a warm place until the butter has melted.
2. Add the rest of the ingredients and keep warm until ready to serve over the pudding.

Vegetable Plum Pudding

To show the discrepancy between social classes in Victorian Britain, here is a recipe from Eliza Acton's book for poor people's Christmas pudding. This recipe is said to have been enough to feed 16 people.

450 g boiled and mashed potatoes	
225 g boiled and mashed carrots	
450 g flour	
225 g suet	
350 g sugar	
450 g currants	
450 g raisins	
2 tsp nutmeg	
2 tsp mixed spice	

½ tsp salt

2 eggs

1 glass of either brandy,
sherry or stout

Method

1. Mix together the mashed, cooked potatoes and the carrots.
2. Mix in the flour and the rest of the ingredients (if adding brandy or spirits, then add 50 g breadcrumbs to the mix).
3. Flour a dampened pudding cloth well and put the mixture into in the middle. Tie tightly.
4. Put into boiling water and boil for 4 hours.

NB. This pudding would probably have been served with a sweet white sauce instead of the usual brandy sauce.

Mrs Beeton's Mincemeat (Fruit Mincemeat)

The Victorians seem to have eaten the old mincemeat pies with meat in them alongside the fruit ones we all know and love today. Mrs Beeton has both mincemeat recipes together as festive pies. They must have had some way of telling the difference between the two types, for it would not have been a very pleasant experience to bite into a mince pie thinking it is going to taste sweet, only to find it had beef in it!

3 large lemons
2 large apples
450 g raisins
450 g currants

| 450 g suet |
| 1 kg moist brown sugar |
| 75 g sliced citron (whole candied peel) |
| 1 teacup of brandy |
| 2 tbsp orange marmalade |

Method

1. Grate the rind of the lemons and squeeze out the juice (boil the remainder of the lemon until it is tender and then chop it very finely and add it to the bowl).
2. Bake the apples after they have been peeled and cored, and then add to the bowl.
3. Add the rest of the ingredients and mix well.
4. Store in jars and it will be ready to use in two weeks.

Mrs Beeton's Christmas Cake

This is a very different cake to the one we know today. The huge amounts of fruit seem to be reserved for the pudding and the mince pies, as this cake is actually a ginger cake with only a little fruit in it. Or perhaps it is a fruity version of our Twelfth Night cake.

1.25 kg flour

250 g melted butter

300 ml cream

300 ml treacle

250 g moist brown sugar

2 eggs

25 g ginger

225 g raisins

1 tsp bicarbonate of soda

1 tbsp vinegar

Method

1. Melt the butter.
2. Put the flour, sugar, ginger and raisins into a bowl.
3. Stir the butter into the dry ingredients with the cream, treacle and whisked eggs and beat the mixture well.
4. Dissolve the soda in the vinegar and add to the mixture.
5. Put the mix in a buttered mould or tin and bake in a moderate oven for 2 hours or until firm to the touch.

Frosted Holly Leaves

A lovely festive decoration. Please note, these are not edible.

Sprigs of holly

Melted butter

Icing sugar and caster sugar mixed

Method

1. Pick the holly leaves from their stalks and dry them near the fire (not too near, or they will shrivel).
2. Dip the leaves in the butter and sprinkle over the mixed sugars.
3. Put them near the heat again to dry, then decorate the table with them or use pins to stick them into the base of a candle. Sit the candle on a large plate, also decorated with the leaves. Do not let the candle burn low enough to touch the leaves or they will catch fire.

Hot Christmas Punch

300 ml rum

300 ml brandy

125 g sugar

1 large lemon

½ tsp nutmeg

600 ml boiling water

Method

1. Rub the sugar over the lemon peel until it has taken all the zest into the sugar.
2. Add the lemon juice mix to the brandy, rum and nutmeg.
3. Add the boiling water and serve.

Bibliography

Armesto, Felipe Fernandez, *Food: A History* (London: Macmillan Ltd, 2001)

Beeton, Mrs, *Mrs Beeton's Book of Household Management*, a first edition facsimile (London: Jonathan Cape Ltd, 1974)

Berriedale-Johnson, Michelle, *The British Museum Cook Book* (London: British Museum Press, 1987)

Drummond, J.C. and Wilbraham, Anne, *The Englishman's Food* (London: Pimlico Ltd, 1939)

Flavel, Sidney, *Menus and Recipes: Cooking the Flavel Way* (London: Sidney Flavel & Co Ltd, 1962)

Glasse, Hanna, *The Art of Cookery Made Easy*, facsimile edition by Karen Hess (Massachusetts: Applewood Books, 1997)

Isitt, Verity, *Take a Buttock of Beef* (Southampton: Ashford Press Publishing, 1987)

Mckendry, Maxime, *Seven Centuries of English Cooking* (London: C. Tinling & Co Ltd, 1973)

Moss, Peter, *Meals Through The Ages* (London: George G. Harrop Ltd, 1958)

Pegge, Samuel (compiler), *The Forme of Cury* (Bibliobazaar Ltd, 2006)

Ray, Elizabeth (compiler), *The Best of Eliza Acton* (Southampton: The Camelot Press Ltd, 1968)

Spurling, Hilary, *Elizor Fettiplaces Receipt Book* (Middlesex: Penguin Books Ltd, 1987)

Index

Basic conversion chart

Liquid, Volume

	Metric	Imperial
1/4tsp		1.2 ml
1/2 tsp		2.5 ml
1 tsp		5.0 ml
1/2 tbsp		7.5 ml
1 tbsp	1/2 fl oz	15 ml
1/8 cup	1 fl oz	30 ml
1/4 cup	2 fl oz	60 ml
1/3 cup	2 1/2 fl oz	80 ml
1/2 cup	4 fl oz	120 ml
2/3 cup	5 fl oz	160 ml
3/4 cup	6 fl oz	180 ml
1 cup	8 fl oz	250 ml

Weight

Imperial	Metric	Temperature °F	°C
1/4 oz	7 g	200	90
1/2 oz	15 g	250	120
1 oz	30 g	300	150
2 oz	55 g	350	180
3 oz	85 g	400	200
4 oz (1/4 lb)	115 g	475	250
8 oz (1/2 lb)	225 g		
16 oz (1 lb)	250 g		

Also in this series

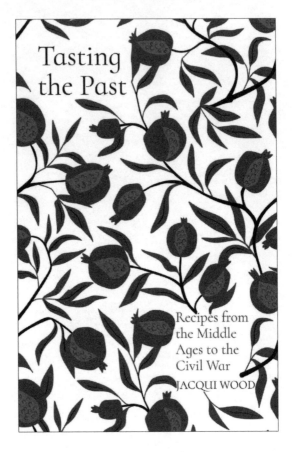

Tasting
the Past

Recipes from
the Middle
Ages to the
Civil War

JACQUI WOOD

9780750992244